THE
Archive Photographs
SERIES

TETTENHALL
AND
PATTINGHAM

Lower Green, Tettenhall in 1906, with St Michael's Church behind the Mitre Inn. This is one of the few scenes in Tettenhall which has hardly changed over the century.

A drawing of Pattingham Church and vicarage in the eighteenth century, before the spire was added to the tower.

THE
Archive Photographs
SERIES

TETTENHALL
AND
PATTINGHAM

Compiled by
Alec Brew

CHALFORD

First published 1997
Copyright © Alec Brew, 1997

The Chalford Publishing Company
St Mary's Mill, Chalford,
Stroud, Gloucestershire, GL6 8NX

ISBN 0 7524 0769 4

Typesetting and origination by
The Chalford Publishing Company
Printed in Great Britain by
Bailey Print, Dursley, Gloucestershire

Other books in The *Archive Photographs* series by Alec Brew
Albrighton and Shifnal
Codsall and Claregate
Staffordshire and Black Country Airfields

The rural tranquillity which separated Tettenhall from its large industrial neighbour, Wolverhampton, at the turn of the century. This is one of two mill pools next to Henwood Lane.

Contents

TETTENHALL ROAD, WOLVERHAMPTON,

Another View in the (BLACK) Country. with or by, from N.A.R.

The road to Tettenhall from Wolverhampton, showing St Jude's Church. The card was written to someone in Somerset who obviously did not think the Black Country could look like this.

Four former Dutch soldiers stationed at Perton during the Second World War on their de-mob. The concrete statue behind was in the original church at RAF Perton beside the entrance road to York's Farm; it was then moved to stand outside the Dutch Church. (G. Spencer)

Introduction

Facing Wolverhampton, on the other side of the valley in which Smestow Brook lies, is the ancient village of Tettenhall. Built on a ridge astride the main Holyhead Road, which used to climb steeply up Old Hill, Tettenhall has always been fiercely independent of its larger neighbour: once in fact and, more recently, only in spirit.

This community spirit encompasses the local large villages of Compton, Tettenhall Wood, Pattingham and Perton, the latter an ancient settlement now much enlarged on the former wartime airfield of RAF Perton, as well as the smaller village of Burnhill Green and the other areas of the Patshull Park Estate.

The area is entirely agricultural and residential in nature, in contrast to the industry of its southern neighbours, and the 220 photographs in this book attempt to rekindle memories of the old Tettenhall Urban District, of Seisdon Rural District, and the people and places which made the area such a tranquil contrast to the fiery holes of the Black Country.

The commanding geographical feature of the area is the escarpment known as Tettenhall Ridge, curving north to become Perton Ridge. It is Tettenhall's fortune and misfortune that this ridge affords such wonderful panoramic views. It was inevitable that the rich industrialists of the Black Country should be attracted to the picturesque rural village of Tettenhall to build their large houses along this ridge, and families such as the Manders, Thorneycrofts, Marstons and Hickmans came to dominate the village with houses there, alongside Wood Road, through Tettenhall Wood, Wightwick and Perton.

Once such families had arrived, it was inevitable that others would follow, and as the suburban sprawl of Wolverhampton spread along the wide tree-lined avenue of the Tettenhall Road and the more westerly Compton Road, it was also inevitable that the intervening fields would vanish under bricks and mortar. Tettenhall Wood and the village of Compton at the foot of Tettenhall Ridge were also joined to the whole. Tettenhall Urban District Council was finally swallowed up by Wolverhampton during the 1960s local government reorganisation and both were then sliced from Staffordshire and flung into the abortive West Midlands County. Even the new boundary of Staffordshire along Yew Tree Lane failed to stop the further expansion of the West Midlands conurbation when the former RAF airfield at Perton was developed as a self-contained 'village', linked by footpath and bus route, if not directly by road, with Wolverhampton.

Only further on does the large village of Pattingham retain its identity, giving some insight into the way that the villages of Tettenhall, Compton, and Tettenhall Wood used to be.

Although now largely a dormitory village, it still caters for the local rural community, the farms and the houses in the local countryside.

When I was born my parents lived in the Slings Cottages on the Pattingham Road at Perton; my father worked on the Wrottesley Estate as a woodman and my first school was the old one at Tettenhall Wood. Since then all these things have gone, and the area has become one for golf courses and large new housing estates. This book tries to remember different, slightly slower days, both for those who knew them then and for those who have moved there since.

A 1949 Guy trolley bus about to ascend the Rock. The route to Tettenhall was always No.1 for Wolverhampton's Corporation Transport Department, though now it is No.501 in the era of the 'West Midlands County'.

One
A Tram Ride to Tettenhall

The road to Tettenhall, or the Tettenhall Road as it starts out, before becoming the Wergs Road and then the Holyhead Road, is the main route from Wolverhampton to the North West. Originally horse drawn coaches followed the road down the hill from High Green, Wolverhampton - or Queen Square as it became - to the old bridge over the canal before making the very steep climb up what later became Old Hill to Tettenhall, and then down the Wrottesley Road through Wrottesley Park.

In the 1820s Thomas Telford cut a new road up the Tettenhall escarpment known as the Rock, and a new bridge was built over the canal. It was along this wide, tree-lined road, that Wolverhampton's premier tram route was laid, with horse drawn and then electric trams which were later replaced by trolley buses and now, motor buses. If someone from the top of the tram below was implanted on the top deck of a No.501 bus today, they would see remarkably few changes along the way, though the clip-clop of the horses' hooves on the cobbles would be noticeably missed.

Around the turn of the century horse drawn trams such as this one operated the route from Queen Square, Wolverhampton, to Tettenhall, though it must have been hard going for the horses up the Rock with a full load of passengers.

Tram No.32 stands ready in the Cleveland Road Depot to undertake the journey to Tettenhall, around 1905.

Queen Square, Wolverhampton in 1908, and the single decker tram is just beginning the descent of Darlington Street towards Tettenhall.

At the bottom of Darlington Street, also in 1908, a tram is just swinging round the corner from Chapel Ash, passing St Mark's Church, which still stands but is now offices.

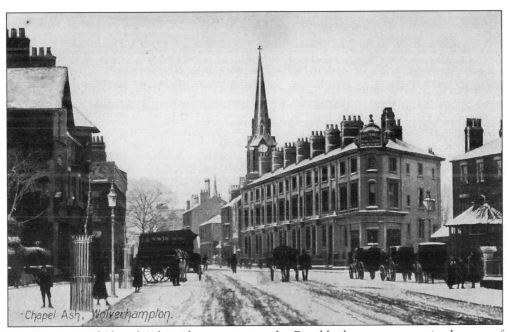

The lower part of Chapel Ash, with no trams in sight. Possibly they are not running because of the snow, although the London & North Western Railway parcel van is delivering.

Just below Chapel Ash, with St Mark's still visible; the road now becomes the Tettenhall Road. All the houses on the right are still there, numbered 1 to 35.

On the corner of Albert Road and Riches Street these two houses, Nos 77 and 79 Albert Road, which were built in 1897, now make up the Queen Victoria Hotel. No one is waiting at the tram stop however.

A tram outside St Jude's Church in 1910, opposite another parcels van, which advertises 'parcels collected and delivered to all parts of the United Kingdon and abroad' - though perhaps not quite as quickly as DHL. The houses on the left, Nos 171-181, are still there.

St Jude's Primary School football team in 1950/51 were possibly regular travellers on the later trolley buses. Teachers, from left to right: Mr Evans and headteacher, Mr Mott. Back row: R. Lewis, Tommy Tannant, Trevor Roberts, Carl Gardner, -?-, ? Gandhy. Seated: Celt Evans, David Healey, -?-, Roger Bannister, John Gough, -?-, ? Shuttleworth.

Just below St Jude's in 1904 and a tram passes some houses which are all still there. The Tettenhall Road is the most photographed road in Wolverhampton, showing as it does a wide tree-lined thoroughfare quite unlike the other main roads into the town. The section by St Jude's was the most popular of all.

Slightly nearer to Tettenhall and the mock half-timbered houses are Nos 106-112, which were built in 1892 and are still to be seen, though the gas light has gone.

This tram is just going by the end of Newhampton Road West. St Jude's, which was built in 1867, is still visible in the background.

The view of the lower part of Tettenhall village from the area of what was to become Crowther Road and before the railway was built. The canal lies just beyond the field of cows.

Thomas Telford thought the road over the new bridge and up the Rock unnecessarily wide and therefore expensive, and so it seems in this view. Even in those days you waited for ages for a tram, and then two came along together.

The block of houses and shops at Newbridge still remains, but the old Newbridge Inn, opposite the tram, has now gone.

An advertisement for one of the shops in Newbridge. The area around the new bridge over the canal, which was built in the 1820s, adopted its name.

View taken from Newbridge looking ~ which is the boundary ~ J

Wolverhampton

A photograph showing Smestow Brook, the boundary between Wolverhampton and Tettenhall. It was navigable for small boats until the canal was built in 1792. The old road ran over the canal bridge to the left and on the other side of the cottages.

The Newbridge Inn was right next to the new canal bridge, from which steamers could be taken to Brewood and Coven. This inn has now gone and the new Newbridge Inn is on the other side of the road, further away from the canal.

The railway, which cuts through the row of houses, was not built until 1920. The end of Tettenhall station platform can be seen through the gap.

The old canal bridge over the Staffordshire and Worcestershire Canal, photographed from the new bridge. Many people pass by each day without knowing it is there, but it can be seen from the top of a bus or a tram.

The 10th Wolverhampton Sea Scouts outside their makeshift headquarters next to the canal at Newbridge in July 1945. The officers saluting the flag are E.W. Williams and R. Buckingham.

Tettenhall & Newbridge Motor Services at the bottom of the Rock, was founded by G.H. Kent in 1929 and is still a major feature of the Tettenhall Road today.

Lower Street, Tettenhall.

The view from the bottom of the Rock down Lower Street in 1906. In the distance a man and child are pulling a sledge towards Lower Green to go sledging, much as they still do on snowy winter days today.

Tettenhall Church.

The view of St Michael's Church, Tettenhall, from Lower Green, or the bottom deck of a tram ascending the Rock.

The view up the Rock from the junction with Old Hill, although it's a trolley bus passing the lodge to Avenue House. This was the type running when the last trolley bus service left Tettenhall on 30 June 1963.

An earlier 3 axle trolley bus just leaving the Upper Green bus stop and about to descend the Rock. Trolley buses began running on the Tettenhall route on 1 January 1929.

Back to the era of the tram, and a double decker is just arriving at the sadly missed 'Swiss Chalet' bus shelter, which had been displayed at the 1902 Exhibition in West Park but was demolished in the 1970s.

One of the many reasons to take a ride to Tettenhall by tram or by bus: the paddling pool on Upper Green, which was opened in 1934, having been a farm pond before that.

The crew of a United Electric Car tram, *c.* 1918, pose at the terminus on Tettenhall Green, before making the journey back to Wolverhampton.

Two

Tettenhall

Tettenhall has been inhabited since at least the Middle Ages, and was reputed to be the site of a battle between the Saxons and Danes. Little more than a village for most of its existence, the Urban District of Tettenhall was formed in 1894. Soon afterwards the age of the commuter began as the first Wolverhampton tram lines were laid to the village and for a short while trains also ran from Tettenhall station to Wolverhampton.

Beginning with rich industrialists who built large houses along Tettenhall Ridge, the area became a dormitory for its larger neighbour, and as the suburbs of Wolverhampton spread down into the Smestow Valley, the two communities eventually coalesced until the 1960s when Tettenhall became part of an enlarged Wolverhampton, which henceforth stretched as far as Yew Tree Lane at the Wergs.

A drawing showing the view from behind Tettenhall Church towards Wolverhampton, its larger neighbour on the other side of the Smestow Valley, with only fields beyond the houses of Lower Street.

On 22 June 1897, this tree was planted on Upper Green in celebration of Queen Victoria's Diamond Jubilee; it is known as the Jubilee Tree.

Upper Green, Tettenhall, at around the turn of the century, before the clock tower was erected. A horse is grazing where the bus stop is today and the woman and girl are standing at the end of Stockwell Road.

The old smithy which stood at the end of Stockwell Road at the top of the Rock, in about 1913.

Tettenhall Pool when it was just a farm pond, with Upper Green Farm in the background. The farmhouse, one of the oldest houses in the village, still stands.

The congregation leaving St Michael's Church at around the turn of the century, strolling home along Church Road.

The view enjoyed by the ladies in the picture above, along Church Road and towards Old Hill. The cottage on the right has now gone.

Waiting to cross the tram tracks on the Rock, the walk back to the village would have been up Old Hill. The lovely cottages on the right have now been demolished.

Nearing the top of Old Hill the Rose and Crown is on the left, and might have proved a temptation after walking up the hill from the church!

A Bible class in the 1890s, in the grounds of Glen Bank, later the Gables, on Wood Road. The lady who gave the class is Charlotte Pearsall Mander, youngest daughter of Samuel Mander. On the left is John Edward Chambers; seated on Miss Mander's right is John Young and on her left are Mr Middleton and Mr Alcock, both of Mill Lane, Wightwick.

The Oaklands was the large house in Regis Road which later became the offices of the Tettenhall Urban District Council, and now includes the library.

The Coronation Day dedication of the clock tower on Upper Green in 1911, with members of the Territorial Army marching by. It was presented by Mr and Mrs Swindley of the Cedars.

Members of the local Territorials at camp at Hindlow, near Buxton, in 1910. The man marked is Dan Brew of Oaken, then 18 years old, who was later to become the ganger in charge of the permanent way on the railway through Tettenhall. Like many others he joined the Territorials because the two week summer camp was a welcome holiday.

The Rock Hotel, alongside Old Hill just before the First World War.

The smoke room and bar of the Rock Hotel in 1907.

The Rock Hotel's bowling green, photographed some time between the World Wars.

Wolverhampton Cricket Club at Tettenhall, with a very recognisable W.G. Grace guesting for one of the teams.

Colonel Thomas Thorneycroft, the well liked and slightly eccentric resident of Tettenhall Towers. The Thorneycrofts, with the Manders, Marstons and the Hickmans, were some of the great families who made their fortunes in Black Country industries and who built large houses on Tettenhall Ridge.

Tettenhall Towers, Wolverhampton.

A game of croquet in front of Tettenhall Towers, Colonel Thorneycroft's residence alongside Wood Road, and now part of Tettenhall College.

The interior of the Towers was very ornate and this is the hall with tiger skin rugs on the floor. There were also assorted weaponry and shooting trophies on the walls.

Colonel Thorneycroft was a great inventor of gadgets; this is his sock and shoe warmer, connected to the central heating system.

A garden party in the grounds of Tettenhall Towers sometime during the 1890s.

Colonel Thorneycroft also organised a carriage driving club; he is seen here ascending his own coach and four.

Colonel and Mr Thorneycroft posing with members of their family outside the Towers.

The officers of the local Territorial Army Regiment at Hindlow Camp, 1910. Back row from left to right: Mr R.W. Lewis, Capt Trench, Lt Lewis, Capt Barlow, Surgeon Lt Hewitt, Capt and Adjt Harden, Capt Holcroft, Lt Clayton, Sims, Smyth, Adam, Cresswell. Seated: Capt McBean, Capt Law, Maj Addenbrooke, Lady Airedale, Mrs T.E. Hickman, Col Waterhouse, Col T.E. Hickman CC, DSO, CB, Mrs Waterhouse, Capt Taylor, Capt Barnett and Capt Lowe. Front row: Lt Parkes, Lt Howl, Lt Joynson, Lt Thursfield.

Lower Street, Tettenhall, in 1903, with the Swan public house to the left. All the houses on the right have now been demolished apart from the first two, which are next to the entrance to St Michael's School.

Children at St Michael's School, Tettenhall, in 1886.

Fifteen years later in 1901, and another group of children from the school pose for the camera.

Church Walk, up from Lower Street to the back of the church, with a butchers shop on the left.

Lower Street by the Swan, decorated for the wedding of the daughter of Mr and Mrs Crane.

A cottage at the bottom of Grotto Lane behind the church, which has now been demolished to make way for an extension to the graveyard.

The lady who was the midwife for the village for many years

A house in Mancroft Road in 1909. Outside are Mrs Helena Nash and her daughter Lucy.

Upper Green in the 1920s. The building to the right of Old Hill was the police station and has long since been demolished for the new block of shops. The building on the left was the Institute and is now Woodville delicatessen.

Upper Green looking towards Wolverhampton during the 1930s. Only the age and the solitariness of the car date the picture.

Home of the Barn Dweller, Tettenhall, Wolverhampton,   *Copyright.*

A barn at the bottom of Danescourt Road, which is now a barn conversion, and was before according to this photograph. In 1929-30 it became a Boys Club, with a snooker table upstairs and a club room downstairs, with the key held by Mr Atkins in the adjoining cottage.

The boys of St Michael's School in 1937. The teachers are Arthur Mould and C.B. Foster. Back row, third from the left is John Morris, and fifth, Frank Lander. Second row, eighth from the left is Malcolm Marple, last is Derek Benson. Third row, on the right is Lionel Rutter. Front row, seventh from the left is Ron Sutton, ninth is Bob Satherwaite and tenth is Jack Holmes, who lived in Blackburn Avenue, Claregate.

43

The Veterans Administration Department Hospital at the bottom of Old Hill, just after the First World War, with some of the nurses gathered in the doorway.

Tettenhall College in 1933 was a private school based on Tettenhall Towers.

TETTENHALL. G.W.

Tettenhall station in the 1920s. The line boasted a passenger diesel railcar service for just seven years and then reverted to goods traffic only.

The 1,000 hp Sunbeam was the first car in the world to exceed 200 mph when it broke the World Land Speed Record in 1929. Especially built with two Matabele aircraft engines, it is shown here at the Gables, Wood Road, the home of John Marston, the founder of the Sunbeam Motor Car Company.

The farm pool on Upper Green being converted to a children's paddling pool in 1934, at the expense of Mr Graham, the proprietor of the *Express and Star*.

Preparations for war in Tettenhall in 1939. Sand bags are being filled to be placed around the council offices. One wonders if these boys were paid for doing the work.

Members of the Women's Auxiliary Police Corps in Tettenhall in 1942.

The officers of the 24th Battalion of the Home Guard, 'C' Company, outside the company headquarters at Stockwell House. In the centre of the front row is Major Trevor-Jones, the commanding officer. The company had platoons based at the Wergs, Wightwick Manor and the New Inns in Lower Street.

A cartoon from the battalion's own official history showing the Local Defence Volunteers, LDVs (or Look, Duck and Vanish) as they first appeared in May 1940.

The entire battalion drawn up on Lower Green in May 1943, on the occasion of the third anniversary of their formation.

The despatch riders on their way from Lower Green to a field opposite Nethy House.

Major Webster, OC 'A' Company (Codsall) saluting as the battalion marches past on Upper Green, past the 3,000 spectators.

An Auxiliary Fire Service tender on Upper Green during the Second World War.

The Tettenhall branch of what was still the National Fire Service in 1947, posing on an old fire engine. The fire station was then near the Dog and Gun.

The firemen with their up to date fire engine, c. 1947. Tettenhall became part of Wolverhampton Fire Service and then part of South Staffordshire, before reverting to Wolverhampton's tender loving care when Tettenhall was absorbed by its big neighbour.

Compton Football Club First XI outside the Fieldhouse pub in Claregate in 1947. The club lead a nomadic existence and their home pitch was often moved.

The Rose and Crown on Old Hill falling into disrepair before its eventual demolition.

Lower Street after the Second World War, with the Swan on the left and the doomed houses on the right.

Prime Minister Harold MacMillan, no doubt telling the people on Tettenhall Upper Green that 'they had never had it so good'.

Pupils at St Michael's School in 1952. The teacher in glasses is Mr Foster. Back row, third from the left is Tony Fownes, fourth, Freddie Akers, seventh, Robert Davies. Second row, fifth from the left is Heather Davies and eighth is Gweneth Sutton. Third row, fourth from the left is Robert Marshall. Front row, third from the left, is Barbara Walters, now Barbara Gardner.

Sports day at St Michael's School in 1953.

The corner of Yew Tree Lane and Wergs Road in 1910.

Wergs Garage in the 1960s when it was still a Volkswagen dealership. It had been bought by the Moseley family in 1958, and they still own it today.

Redhouse Farm in Redhouse Road, one of many farms in the Tettenhall area which are no more, as the village has turned from a rural community into the most affluent suburb of Wolverhampton.

An aerial view of Tettenhall College taken on 7 September 1948, showing Wood Road in the foreground and Henwood Road, the railway and canal all in close proximity behind. Note the tennis courts just off Newbridge Crescent and the ploughing going on in the area which is now Compton Park.

at a Birmingham Nature centre ... ...tume
...ctorian Photographer of the Year (to 7 June)

Soap opera

by David Vincent

Unlucky-in-love Sinbad looses out once again

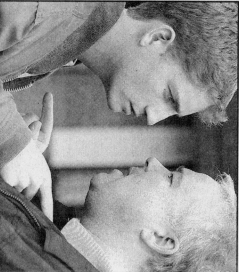

Tinhead and Sinbad – at loggerheads once more

NEIGHBOURS (BBC1)

Karl is stunned to discover their affair and Jack Foster gets the sack. Toadie's ill-judged attempts to impress have dangerous repercussions and Darren realises that living under the same roof as him isn't quite as much fun as he'd anticipated. Ramsay Street waits for news as Madge takes a serious tumble down the house steps while Lance tells Amy they're through but finds she doesn't give up that easily.

EASTENDERS (BBC1)

Albert Square's younger residents watch Mick's band play live, giving Huw the opportunity to use his Celtic charm on Ruth, who seems only too willing to co-operate. A vicious gang attempt to scare Peggy into revealing the whereabouts of their arch enemy, George Palmer, but passer-by Frank leaps in to save the

handed. Travis is horrified to discover evidence of drug abuse in the house and tracks down Gypsy to find out who the culprit is. He also reassesses his relation-ship with Joel, the big

little games, shocking Des with the news that she's changed her mind about the baby. Sally blows her top with Kevin, aghast to learn he's planning to hand her inheritance over to

promise after consuming one too many alcoholic drinks and Maria feels left out as the girls make plans for the barbecue. Chris is furious to discover Jamie's modem is responsible for a rocketing phone bill and the youngster causes further concern by return-ing from school with only one shoe.

BROOKSIDE (C4)

Tin-head determines to help Carmel with her financial problems but her decision to move away from the Close signals the end for her and unlucky-in-love Sinbad. The Farnham household receives the test results and Marcus makes Louise's day by inviting her along to his live radio inter-view mesmerising the teen-ager with his charisma. Jimmy applies for more teaching jobs to keep Jackie happy.

EMMERDALE (ITV)

Class war rages in Emmer-

Nick Fletcher

...about 1810 and ... would have been worth m... than £1,000...

However, this is an early 20th century replica, still as beautiful but worth only about £200.

The classic design of these Regency convex mirror has remained popular for almost 200 years and you can still buy modern versions.

A good example from the mid-Victorian period is going to cost between £150 and £200.

The Cheval mirror is a floor standing

...increasing demand for small mirror both for hanging on the wall, and of a tiltable design, meant to stand on a dressing table or chest of drawers. These are probably the most popular sellers within the antiques trade, small and compact, often very attractively designed, and can be moved around very easily.

England, will turn 50 in October, 1998.

4. Fictional milk maid and murderess; Hardy's creation; they caught up with me at Stonehenge.

ANSWERS: 1, Dr David Livingstone; 2, Erich Honecker; 3, Trevor Brooking, 4, Tess of the d'Urbervilles.

This week's photograph is of the Boat Inn, Compton, taken in 1926. The photograph was supplied by Mr Frank W. Webberley of Finchfield whose grandfather on his mothers side was licensee of the Boat Inn for many years.

Bridge

ANSWERS:

...cky enough to win
...ners who visit the
...il store and spend
...ugh £5 gift voucher to

F/FM 9d, 1998.

Three
Tettenhall Wood

Tettenhall Wood used to be known as Kingsley Wood and was actually part of the parish of Kinver. The village grew up around the top of Compton Holloway, the first road up Tettenhall Ridge west of Old Hill in Tettenhall. With its own school and church it remained quite independent of its larger neighbour at the other end of Wood Road until well into this century, but eventually the inevitable happened and the two communities merged, just as they would jointly both merge with Wolverhampton.

WOOD ROAD AND INSTITUTE, TETTENHALL.

The Tettenhall Wood Institute was opened in 1893 and provided reading, bagatelle and smoke rooms for the local working men. It is still in use as a community centre but both buildings by the crossroads, just beyond the horse and trap, have long gone.

Wood Road looking towards Tettenhall, around 1905. The house, which is still there, was the lodge for Wood House, the home of the Hickman family. All the large houses on the other side of Wood Road lay at the top of the Ridge, with fine views towards Wolverhampton.

Mrs Tertins Mander, who later became Lady Mander, ready for a sleigh ride outside the Mount in 1905. She was Canadian by birth and so the furs and mode of transport might well have brought back memories of home.

The same view as that opposite, but taken in the summer. The fence on the left has replaced the earlier hedge. The trees along Wood Road provided a tunnel-like canopy of leaves.

A Tettenhall Wood family just after a wedding at Christ Church. The brand new Mrs Alcock is flanked by her husband and his brother, and Maggie Riley is the younger of the bridesmaids.

Henry Malin, the gamekeeper for Sir Charles Mander at the Mount, around 1900. He lived at the Slings Cottages, Perton, and had previously been at Ragley Hall.

David Lloyd George outside the Mount in 1918, with members of the Mander family.

Queen Mary passing through Tettenhall Wood in July 1939, after visiting Lady Mander at the Mount. Local people are gathered round the crossroads outside the Institute.

Class II at Tettenhall Wood School, Christ Church, in the 1920s.

Class IV at the same time. The original school which opened in 1844 is now Tettenhall Wood Library, and the enlarged school over the road is now a special school.

Tettenhall Wood School football team in 1938. Back row from left to right: Derek Middleton, J. Pullen, Allan Crane. Seated: Neville Lawler, John Bright, Kenneth Howell, James Hunter, Robert Pinches. Front row: Alfred Tooth, Thomas Chapman, Roy Hyatt.

A view down Compton Holloway from the old Christ Church Vicarage gardens, *c.* 1905. The carriage is being driven by Mr Bott, the coachman to Mr Underhill of Stockwell End.

Mr A. Nicholls' butchers shop in Tettenhall Wood, which has now gone.

Two of the great pioneers of British aviation in the ballroom of the Mount Hotel in 1967 at the retirement party for Fred Crocombe, on the left. He was Chief Designer for Boulton Paul Aircraft and before that, Blackburn and General Aircraft, designing the Beverley amongst other aircraft. Handing him the camera is J.D. North, Chairman of Boulton Paul, who had joined the company in 1917 as Chief Engineer and had been Chief Designer to Grahame White Aviation in 1913.

Four
Compton and Wightwick

Compton was a small, rural village at the bottom of the Holloway, the steep road down Tettenhall Ridge, and therefore the lower neighbour of Tettenhall Wood. It lay at the junction of Henwood Lane which ran to Lower Green, Tettenhall, and the Wolverhampton to Bridgnorth Road. Both the Staffordshire and Worcestershire Canal and the GWR Wolverhampton to Stourbridge railway run side by side through the village, which remained basically a rural community.

As the century progressed the march of houses built down the Compton Road from Wolverhampton eventually engulfed the village and the last farm was swallowed up in the 1960s, so that Compton is now just another suburb of its big neighbour.

Wightwick is a community scattered along the next road cut up Tettenhall Ridge, called Wightwick Bank. It has one pub, the Mermaid, at the bottom of the hill next to the Bridgnorth Road, and one on the Perton Road, the Fieldhouse, near the top of the hill, but it has no church or shops.

The road into Compton village from Wolverhampton on a snowy day in 1905. The house on the right was just over the brow of Compton Hill past the Cedars, but is no longer there.

A little further down the hill the Boat Inn later became a private house and was demolished in the 1950s. After the First World War there used to be a German helmet, complete with spike, in the front window, which used to fascinate local children leaning on the railings.

A few yards further on and the little cottage on the right is still there today, but Lodge Farm and Compton Farm in the background have now gone.

A photograph taken from under where the railway bridge was built in 1925. The wagon is just approaching the canal bridge and the Leonard T. Law coal wharf is on the right.

The centre of Compton in the 1920s. All these buildings are now gone, the ones on the right replaced by the Oddfellows pub, the ones ahead by new shops.

The rear of the white buildings on the previous photograph, showing John Turton's coal barge from Gospel Oak, Tipton, tied up at Compton Wharf around 1900.

Compton Lock, which was the first built by James Brindley on the Staffordshire and Worcestershire Canal, which he completed in 1772. It took boats to the highest level of the canal. The Beech family hired out rowing boats from the little white cottage, which has now gone.

An unusual view looking up Compton Holloway around the turn of the century.

The more common view of the Holloway looking down from near the bend, showing the green fields which stretched towards Wolverhampton.

69

WIGHTWICK, NEAR WOLVERHAMPTON.

A view of the Mermaid Inn at Wightwick, with Wightwick Manor above. The three children in the foreground, in Mill Lane, are the Twentymen children from Compton Farm, probably walking back from church.

The Alcock family lived in Mill Lane, Wightwick, and this is Mr and Mrs Alcock's wedding picture. Mr Riley is the man with the beard and Maggie Riley is the bridesmaid seated on the right.

Wightwick Bank has been widened since
this photograph was taken at the turn of
the century, but it remains as steep.

Wightwick Manor, which is not quite as old as it looks having been built by Theodore Mander
in 1887. It was given to the National Trust in 1937.

This is Mrs Holt and her children, around the turn of the century. They lived in a Victorian semi-detached cottage near the top of Mill Lane, Wightwick, and Mr Holt worked as a gamekeeper for the Mander family. The boys' names were Arthur and Harold.

The Fieldhouse at Wightwick, looking towards Mount Road, around 1910. The cottages in the distance still exist.

The smithy in front of the Mermaid Inn being demolished to widen the Bridgnorth Road and provide a car park. The bowling green at the side of the inn also became part of the car park.

A panoramic view of Compton taken in the 1950s. The road to Wolverhampton is straight ahead passing under the railway bridge. The new Oddfellows is on the right, but the houses on the left have still to be demolished.

The railway through Tettenhall and Compton was finished in 1925, and for nearly all of its existence the ganger in charge of the line as far as Baggeridge Junction was Dan Brew, seen here on his motor trolley in Wombourne station, in the 1950s.

A steam train can be seen beyond the Swan Inn, on the right. The cottages behind the Swan have now been replaced by shops. The small shops on the left have been replaced by a hideous new block.

Compton Football Club First and Second XIs in 1947. They are posing in the sand hollow at the bottom of the Holloway (hence its name), on the site of the current Compton Social Club. In the panoramic view above, the later bowling green is on the same spot.

One of the most photographed spots in the area: one of the two mill pools in Henwood Lane at the Compton end, where the Boys Club in now situated. This is an almost unbelievably rural scene compared to that of the present.

The other pool in Henwood Lane, looking towards Tettenhall, and at a different time of year.

The start of Henwood Lane, later Road, in Compton, *c.* 1912. Only the first two houses on the right still exist, together with the distant terrace.

Henwood Farm, which lay next to Henwood Lane, was one of several farms in Compton: a rural community which has now been totally swallowed up by the urban sprawl of Wolverhampton.

Percy Kyte next to his Dodge coal lorry just after the Second World War. He ran his coal business from Wightwick Wharf.

Mrs Evelyn Kyte, Percy's wife, at their house in Mill Lane, the Ferns, during one of the parties she used to give for the old people in the district. Mrs Barrington is standing next to her.

A view of the prefabricated houses on Henwood Road, from Compton Hill. These prefabs still stand of course, but most have been completely rebuilt and brick-clad.

West View Cottage in Compton, with Compton Lock just behind, looking towards the new houses which have 'sprouted' all over Tettenhall Ridge.

Compton Farm, taken from the railway in December 1969, just as it was about to be pulled down to make way for yet more houses.

Five

Perton

Although Perton is now thought of as being a new estate built on the former wartime airfield, there was of course a much older, though smaller community in the region. Much of the area of Perton covers the estate of Wrottesley Hall, the seat of Lord Wrottesley, and most of the farms in the area once belonged to him. However it was along the Pattingham Road, on Perton Ridge, where most of the scattered housing was built, attracted by the magnificent views across the Staffordshire countryside.

Aviation came to the area during the First World War when the Fern Fields, alongside the Pattingham Road, were used as a Relief Landing Ground for No.38 (Home Defence) Squadron of the Royal Flying Corps, and the same field was used whenever barnstormers and flying circuses came to the area between the World Wars. However, when an RAF airfield was built at Perton during the Second World War it was on Lord Wrottesley's land, nearer to Wolverhampton. Used as a satellite airfield for the training bases at Shawbury, Tern Hill and Wheaton Aston, RAF Perton closed shortly after 1945 and became the site of the huge new Perton Estate in the late 1970s.

A water colour of the ruins of Perton Hall, which was completed in 1820.

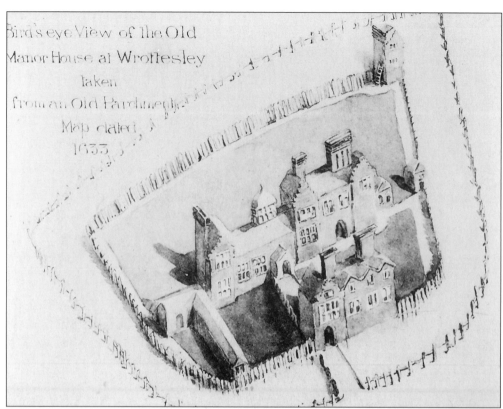

A drawing of the old moated manor at Wrottesley taken from an old parchment map dated 1633. Wrottesley Hall was later built on the same site. By 1678 the Wrottesley family had acquired the manor, which included the village of Oaken.

The rear of Wrottesley Hall before the disastrous fire of 1897. It had been built in the 1690s, but after the fire it lay in ruins for a quarter of a century.

A drawing of Arthur, the third Lord Wrottesley, at the time of the fire. His son, the fourth Lord, was a little eccentric and disliked having his photograph taken.

The front of Wrottesley Hall after it was rebuilt on the old foundations in 1923, now mostly single storey. The estate was sold on the death of the fourth Lord Wrottesley and the fifth Lord went to live in South Africa.

A section of the old Wolverhampton to Shrewsbury Road, which used to cut through Wrottesley Park, after coming up Old Hill, Tettenhall, and then down the Wrottesley Road. When the Rock was cut up Tettenhall Ridge, the new road was built to the east of the old one, rejoining the old route north of Wrottesley Hall. The Perton part of it is now a footpath.

Some Perton ladies who appear to be resting from potato picking. Last on the right is Mrs Jenny Walker, but whether the lane named after her is the one in the background is not known. Back row from left to right: Mrs Howell, Mrs Sargent, Mrs Jane Guest, Mrs Jenny Walker. Front row: Mrs Monckton, Mrs Monckton (snr), Martha Davies, Rosie Sargent, Mrs Davies.

Mrs Malin and her daughter, Alice Elizabeth, outside one of the Slings Cottages on the Pattingham Road, before 1916. The Slings were unusual in being four cottages built north, south, east and west, just opposite the Fern Fields overlooking Slings Wood. They were owned by the Wrottesley Estate and when I was born my father, John Brew, had just taken a job as woodman on the estate because this very cottage came with the job.

In 1941 RAF Perton was completed, but the accommodation units were taken over and extended by the Princess Irene Brigade of the Dutch Army. This was the headquarters building, located next to the Holyhead Road. After the war it became a private house and was then incorporated into a residential home.

Queen Wilhelmina of the Netherlands came to inspect her troops at Perton, and is shown here presenting them with their colours.

Prince Bernhard of the Netherlands (with the swagger stick) is shown at Perton inspecting the Dutch troops under training. The Princess Irene Brigade later fought in France and took part in the liberation of their own country.

During the Second World War York's Farm, just to the north of Perton, put one of the first combine harvesters into use. It was not self-propelled and is shown here being towed by a Fordson tractor, with the two York brothers operating it.

The Dutch Camp at Perton covered quite a wide area; this is an aerial view of York's Farm just after 1945 showing some of the many military buildings surrounding it. The large one on the left was a drill hall and the one with a water tower was one of three ablution blocks. The barn in the foreground has now been converted into two houses and all these buildings can be seen from the first roundabout at the entrance to the Perton Estate.

A group of displaced persons arriving at Perton in 1947 to be housed in the former Dutch Camp. The Army officer on the right supervising their arrival is Major S. Spencer. A former officer in the German Army who served under Rommel, he made his way to Aberdeen at the end of the Second World War and joined the British Army. After two years back in Germany he was transferred to Shrewsbury. (G. Spencer)

Former members of the Dutch Army on their de-mob at Perton. They are standing outside one of the ablution blocks at York's Farm. (G. Spencer)

Compton Football Club in 1947 shown on a field at York's Farm, Perton, which they used for a while. Back row from left to right: Denis Hulme, Jimmy Carter, ? Tooth, Neville Lawler, Maurice Stewart. Front row: Kenny Howell, -?-, -?-, Teddy Turner, M. Dalton, Percy Kyte.

The last airman at Perton, the Pole, Vladek Barela (in the flying jacket), about to leave on his motorbike in 1958 on his way to America. The lady is Mrs Maria Spencer and the two little boys are her sons; they were moving into his hut, No.59, from the hut next door. The other two men are unknown. (G. Spencer)

The first school at Perton was appropriately called Perton First School, and this is the original staff in May 1981. Back row from left to right: Jackie Sharp, Liz Darling, Anne Allman, Georgie Savage, Fred Wiltshire, Irene Russell, Sally Davies, Judy Reynolds, Bill Davies. Front row: Marion Jones, Karen Paul, Roz Bamber, Mel Billings, Phil Dennis, Chris Emslie, Sue Wade. On the floor: Lyn Booth and Sandra Chambers.

Perton First School June Fair in 1985, and headteacher Mel Billings has his shower cap tested.

Perton First School Chess Team in July 1985 after reaching the National Finals. From left to right: James Matthews, John Service, Jaimal Mistry, Mr Billings (who had taught them all to play), Matthew Ashmore and Philip Pinfold. They had been the Wolverhampton U-10 League, U-11 Knock Out Cup winners and English Northern Zone U-9 winners.

The official opening ceremony for Sandown First School, Perton, on 21 June 1984. From left to right: Deaconess Sheila Finn, Mr Norris Cooke (Chairman of Staffordshire Schools Sub-committee), Mr G. Williams (chairman of governors), Miss V.A. Yeoman (headteacher), and David Johnson making the presentation.

The original staff at Sandown. From left to right: Pauline Foster, Liz Allfield, Katherine Ferdinand, Jenny Smith, Jeanette Gardiner, Pam Swallow, Jane Hall, Sue Bowers, Irene Kingston, Eva Viney.

Some angels from the Sandown reception class, Christmas 1983.

The Perton Judo Club which used Sandown First School for a while, until the Community Centre was built.

Six

Pattingham

A large village serving the local rural community for many centuries, Pattingham has not escaped the consequences of its nearness to Wolverhampton, and dormitory housing estates have filled it out but in a way which has not hugely altered the village.

The centre of the village, with the church, the Pigot Arms, school, shops and playing field, still looks out on a vista of fields and woods towards the distant Wrekin. The High Street, though smarter than it was, is still recognisable in photographs from the turn of the century. The new houses all seem to have been built 'behind the scenes' and have not ruined the character of the village, as they have in so many others. Only the awful 1960s block of shops in the centre looks out of place. Out in the countryside, farming and the large estate of Patshull Park dominate the landscape as they always have.

A drawing of St Chad's Church, Pattingham, done in 1796 before the spire was built and the building was enlarged in the nineteenth century. A rather different design of gate is evident.

St Chad's Church, 1874, after the spire had been erected in 1871. It was paid for by Lord Dartmouth of Patshull, as a memorial to his father.

The Reverend William George Greenstreet was the clergyman at Pattingham from 1846 to 1900, and responsible for much of the restoration and enlargement of St Chad's, including its finances.

The lych gate to Pattingham Church, looking much as it does today.

The bellringers at St Chad's, *c.* 1910. Second from the right on the back row is John Law.

The back of the vicarage in 1911, showing Revd Alfred Thomas Greenstreet, the son of William George, and his successor as vicar from 1900 to 1927. He is having a rest from a strenuous game of croquet.

High Street, Pattingham.

The top of the High Street, Pattingham, showing Pattingham Stores on the right.

The heart of Pattingham, 1914, was then called the Bull Ring, with the Pigot Arms dominating the scene.

Two thatched cottages in Morrell Brook Lane. The nearest housed the York family at the time, with George Bowker, the village pig butcher in the second. He kept his own pigs in a couple of sties a short distance further on.

Newgate, or the Wolverhampton Road as it is more commonly known today. The house on the right is still evident, but the next one has gone.

Westbeech Road with the two schools on the right. All these tall trees have gone and the field on the left is now of course the playing field.

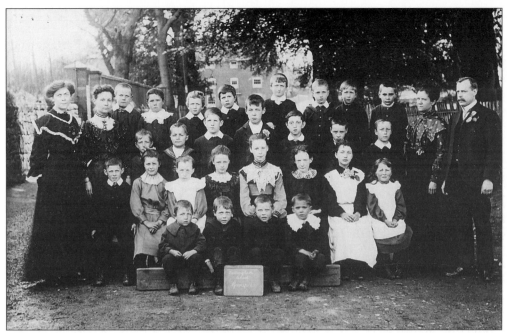

Group I at Pattingham School in 1906. The teacher on the right is Mr Buckley.

Class IV at Pattingham School in the 1920s. At least one of the children is known to be a Law, but as there was more than one Law family in Pattingham, there are probably others. Pattingham has never been very Law-less!

Clive Road near to the centre of Pattingham, with May's Corner on the right - so-called
because Mr May lived there.

Joe Law showing two of his horses at Pattingham Show, which was held on the Rudge Road.

Bert and Sadie Law with their daughter Betty outside a cottage on the Clive Road. It is still there and looks almost identical seventy years later, including the railings.

A different view of the top of Pattingham High Street. Note the tricycle waiting outside the stores.

Seated is John Law, the tenant of Moor Lane Farm, Pattingham, from 1917. His father and uncle had been machinists in the area, hiring threshing machines and the like to the local farmers. Standing behind him is Albert Edwards who was the best man at his wedding. The name of the lady with the hair-do is unknown, unfortunately.

The Law's threshing machine which was pulled by horses and steam driven; a spark from the fire-box eventually set light to the thresher and burnt it out. From left to right: George Law, Fred Russell, Mr Bowker, -?-, Francis Law, -?-, George Pritchard. The dogs were to kill the rats and mice which came out of the stack.

A cottage on the Clive Road on the outskirts of Pattingham, which is now called Birdhouse Cottage and has been almost doubled in size.

Some gamekeepers in the area before the First World War, believed to be seen here at Mere Oak Farm. Second from the right is Jesse Weston, with Henry Malin to his left; in front is Annie Weston, who later emigrated to America.

Jesse and Nancy Weston lived and worked at Mere Oak. The children are, from left to right: John, Samuel (born 1901, and who later worked at Hollies Farm), Anne, William and George.

Mr Skelcher, who was the gamekeeper at
Mere Oak at the turn of the century, with a
fair bag of pheasants on the ground behind.

One of the Law family of Pattingham, whose
first name is not known, proudly showing off
her new bicycle and cycling outfit. Happily
her dog is better behaved than Mr Skelcher's
and is posing nicely for the camera.

John Earl Titley of West End House in 1912, with his two grandchildren, Jack Titley and Jean Russell.

The bottom end of the High Street in Pattingham, before the First World War. Many of the cottages are still there.

Harry Law, son of John Law of Moor Lane Farm, showing two of their horses at Pattingham Show, held in a field off the Rudge Road.

The first of four large properties between Pattingham and Albrighton, pictured when they were all sold by Lord Dartmouth in 1918. This is Whiston Hall, the nearest to Whiston Cross.

Whiston Grange, just off the road from Albrighton to Burnhill Green.

This is the house of Little Whiston Farm, which stands alongside the Burnhill Green Road.

The house on the left is Cosford Grange, with Cosford Grange Farm alongside. The house has now been split into two and the encircling verandah has been removed. Today RAF Cosford airfield is immediately alongside.

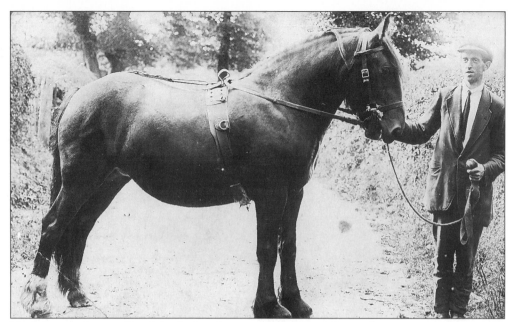

Harry Law with one of his father's shire horses in Moor Lane, Pattingham.

Harry Law, even more proudly showing off a different mode of transport, his brand new bicycle, while wearing his Sunday suit and hat.

Pattingham Peace Celebrations in 1920. A large proportion of the village's population is pictured next to the lych gate to the church, with most of the former soldiers wearing their uniform.

Dorothy Law, the daughter of Joe Law, standing in Clive Road, ready for the May Day celebrations.

The Girl's Friendly Society outside the parish hall at the time of their production of *The Wedding of the Painted Doll* in 1932. The 'policeman' is Nancy Law (later Nancy Caddick).

Another Girl's Friendly Society production, *c.* 1937. Back row from left to right: Ruth Taylor, Jim Nock, Isobel Lloyd, Peggy Nock, Sally Noakes, Annie Ray, Nancy Law, Doris Morgan, Gladys Inett, Olive Johnson, -?-, Ivy Newby, George Edwards. Middle row: -?-, Barbara Sargent, -?-, Kathy Ray, Dorothy Scriven, -?-, Vera Bacchus, -?-, Alwyn Evans, Browny Johnson, Jack Taylor. Front row: Lily Johnson, Nellie Lloyd, Pru Lloyd, -?-, -?-, -?-, -?-, Barbara Taylor, Janet Edwards, Alice Brooks, Flossie French, Edna Monckton, Charlie Edwards.

The Elms on the Clive Road, which was owned by Major Wilson of Ackleton and lived in by Miss Perks, his housekeeper. It was knocked down to make way for a housing estate.

Pepperhill, a large house above Patshull, invisible from the road. The 'fountain' in the foreground came from Patshull Park.

Pattingham football team were the winners of the Shipley and District League in 1930/1, as well as the Fox Cup and the Start Challenge. Back row from left to right: Albert Monckton, Harold Ray, George Russell, -?-, ? Dimmock, Harold Taylor, Sam Glassey, Jack Speade, Jack Taylor. Front row: Charlie Harley, -?-, Jack Stanley, -?-, -?-, -?-, Mr Bullock.

Clive Farm's milk van decorated for either the coronation or the jubilee in the 1930s. Note that the milk was organic - 'free from all preservatives' - and the farm's telephone number was Pattingham 9.

The imposing gateway to Patshull House, the seat of Lord Dartmouth, and before that the Pigot family.

St Mary's Church, Patshull, one of the buildings nestling by Patshull House. Built in 1742-3, it is now looked after by the Churches Conservation Trust and occasional services are still held there.

Queen Mary at Patshull Park, seated with the Earl and Countess of Dartmouth with their daughters behind, Lady Barbara Legge on the left and Lady Josceline Legge.

During the Second World War Patshull Park was used at a training ground by the 24th Battalion of the Home Guard (Tettenhall and Codsall). This is 'B' Company from Wombourne in 1941, emulating Corporal Jones of *Dad's Army*.

This is Captain Collard of 'B' Company demonstrating a Northover Projector at Patshull, also in 1941.

National Fire Service members from Codsall and Pattingham in the garden of the Pigot Arms in 1941. Back row from left to right: Norman Harris, Len Handy, Harold Ray, Charlie Law, ? Bentley, Bill Smith, Stan Bentley, Tom Price, John Strong, Charlie Pritchard, Bert Tooth, -?-. Middle row: all unknown. Front row: Tony Taylor, Leslie Williamson, Clifford Rowley.

The men and women of the National Fire Service in Pattingham during the Second World War.

Food being cooked in Pattingham Stores bakehouse ready for the harvest supper in the parish halls, just after 1945. From left to right: Mrs Monckton, Doris Pugh, Gladys Inett, Vera Gittings, Mary Bradford, Millie Gittings, Nancy Caddick, Revd Prime, Arthur Inett, Joe Caddick and the boy is Grahame Bull.

Mrs Edwards, who kept Pattingham Post Office, just after the end of the Second World War, flanked by Doris Pugh and Bill Pugh, who was the butler at Rudge Hall.

Nancy Caddick, with cat, and Doris Pugh outside the post office where they worked.

Threshing wheat in a field next to the Fox at Shipley in September 1949. Charlie Law is sitting on the tractor, echoing the work done by the Law family as shown on page 105.

Planting potatoes by hand in Patshull Park in April 1951. On the left are Doug Lane and Bill Reynolds.

IT'S A PLEASURE

Brothers Alfred and William Price, of Pattingham, have had, between them, almost 100 years behind the anvil in their father's blacksmiths shop. Their day's work begins early but not, as would be expected, in the blacksmiths shop, for they are also the village postmen. Alfred began delivering the mails 39 years ago, brother Bill followed his example some years later and can only claim 25 years service with the post office. An average day sees them leave their home at 6.30 astride their bicycles. Mails are collected at the post office, and delivered for seven or eight miles around Pattingham. Back at the smithy at 10.30 they change uniform for old clothes and become blacksmiths once again.

The Price brothers, who were both village blacksmiths and postmen for many years, as detailed in the newspaper article.

Scriven's shop on the left and the post office on the right, just before being pulled down in the 1960s. This terrace was on the site of the present new block of shops.

Bert and Polly Brazier and their prize dahlias at Nurton Hill in the 1960s.

The road into Pattingham, more or less as it appears today, with Joe Caddick's cottage on the left, behind which he had his nursery at that time.

The author and his mother enjoying the wonderful view on Perton Ridge in 1951, when we lived in Slings Cottages; possibly discussing a future book?

The book began with a tram ride to Tettenhall, and this is the bus back to Wolverhampton waiting to leave from Pattingham Church. The driver was Norman Wedge and the conductor was William Stockford. Both were regulars on the route from 1956 to 1967.

Acknowledgements

I have to thank two organisations for a substantial number of the photographs used in this book. Firstly, Peter Leigh and the Pattingham Local History and Civic Society, and secondly, Geoff Hancock, who is almost a one man Tettenhall Historical Society. It was from his marvellous *History of Tettenhall* that I gleaned much of the information in this book.

I drew once more on the postcard collection amassed by my own grandmother, Mrs Jane Brew, and the marvellous postcard collections of Harry Blewitt and Mrs B. Walker.

I have also to thank a large number of people who lent me their photographs and their time, and I hope the following includes them all: Leah and John Brew, Peter Brew, Joe Caddick, Carl and Barbara Gardner, Jack Holmes, Les Jordan, Mr and Mrs Percy Kyte, Harry Law, Mrs Middleton, Derek Middleton, Perton First School, Mr James Pinches, Cyril Plimmer, Sandown First School, Andy Simpson, Mrs Sylvia Rogers, Norman Wedge, Miss York and, not least, the much neglected Wendy Matthiason.